DINOSAURS
AND PREHISTORIC CREATURES

by Michael Teitelbaum

THE FACTS ABOUT DINOSAURS

The Rourke Corporation, Inc.
Vero Beach, FL 32964

Library of Congress Cataloging-in-Publication Data
Teitelbaum, Michael.
    Dinosaurs and prehistoric creatures / by Michael Teitelbaum.
        p.   cm. — (The Facts about dinosaurs)
    ISBN 0-86593-355-3
    1. Dinosaurs—Juvenile literature. [1. Dinosaurs.] I. Title. II. Series.
QE862.D5T42   1994
567.9'1—dc20   93-50056
                                                                      CIP
Printed in the USA   AC

CONTENTS

ANKYLOSAURUS
(ang-KILE-uh-sawr-us)

Ankylosaurus was the largest, heaviest, and most well-defended of the **Ankylosaur** (meaning "fused lizard") family of dinosaurs. Thirty-two feet long, and weighing five tons, it was the "tank" of the prehistoric world.

This plant-eater had plates of armor that covered its back, sides, limbs, and skull. But unlike the similar-looking **Stegosaurus**, the Ankylosaurus's armor was not attached to its skin. Instead, it was attached directly to the dinosaur's skeleton.

Even the giant meat-eaters could not break through Ankylosaurus's armor. Ankylosaurus would lie flat on the ground, hiding its soft stomach from attackers. Its tail ended in a bony club that made an excellent weapon when swung at an enemy.

Ankylosaurus had to spend the whole day eating in order to satisfy its hunger.

4

NOTHOSAURUS
(no-tho-SAWR-us)

Nothosaurus was a reptile that lived about 210 million years ago, during the **Triassic** Period. Nothosaurus made its home on the shores of Tethys, where Poland is today.

Paleontologists have found that the use of its powerful legs and strong tail made Nothosaurus a very strong swimmer.

The female laid her eggs on land. Many **fossils** of young Nothosauruses have been found in what were once caves. Caves were perhaps the safest place to lay eggs since few creatures lived in caves.

Nothosaurus had sharp, pointed teeth which made its jaws into a fish trap.

STEGOSAURUS
(STEG-uh-sawr-us)

This large **herbivore** had two rows of big, bony plates on its back. These plates stood up, unlike the flat armor of the **Ankylosaurus**. Some scientists believe that these plates controlled the temperature of the dinosaur's body. Others believe that they protected Stegosaurus from meat-eating dinosaurs.

Stegosaurus defended itself by lashing out with its tail. The tail contained four very sharp spikes, which made it an excellent weapon.

This dinosaur's front legs were only half the size of its back legs. Its skull was long and narrow and its teeth were weak, so it ate only the softest of plants.

Even though Stegosaurus was 30 feet long and weighed two tons, it had a brain the size of a walnut.

8

DIMETRODON
(dye-MET-ruh-don)

Dimetrodon means "two-sized tooth." It got this name because it had teeth of two different sizes. This ten-foot-long meat-eater was a member of the **Spinosaurid** family, which had long bones that stuck up from their backs.

Attached to these bones was a piece of skin that stood three feet off of Dimetrodon's back and looked like a sail on a sailboat. Rival males often used these sails to threaten each other.

However, the main use for the sails was to regulate Dimetrodon's body temperature. At dawn, it stood sideways to catch the sun's rays and warm its body. This helped it get a jump on its cold-blooded prey. At midday, Dimetrodon turned its great sail away from the sun to get rid of excess heat.

Because the sails on their backs were very vulnerable to damage, Dimetrodon did very little actual fighting.

10

DIPLODOCUS
(dih-PLOD-uh-kus)

Diplodocus means "double beam." Its name came from the small bones underneath its backbone. These small bones had two larger beam-like bones attached to them. One bone ran forward toward its head, the other ran back toward its tail.

Diplodocus was one of the longest dinosaurs that ever lived. It sometimes grew to be over 90 feet long. Its tail alone measured 45 feet.

Diplodocus was one of the **Titanosaurs**. This was a group of **Sauropods** that all had long, narrow skulls and nostrils high on their heads. Other Titanosaurs include **Alamosaurus** and **Algoasaurus**.

Diplodocus had skin that looked like leather and a tail that looked like an enormous whip.

12

MAMENCHISAURUS
(mah-MEN-chee-sawr-us)

This Sauropod was a close relative of the more well-known **Diplodocus** and **Apatosaurus**. Its fossils were discovered in an area of China called Mamenchi. That's where it got its name.

Mamenchisaurus was about 72 feet long. Its huge neck contained 19 **vertebrae**. From its shoulders to its tiny head, this plant-eater's neck measured an amazing 36 feet, half its total length.

Some scientists believe it used its enormous neck to reach very high branches on tall trees. Others believe that Mamenchisaurus spent most of its life in rivers and ponds, sweeping its long neck around to feed from vegetation on the banks.

Mamenchisaurus had the longest neck of any dinosaur that ever lived.

14

PROTOCERATOPS
(pro-toe-SAIR-uh-tops)

Protoceratops is the earliest-known member of the **Ceratopsian** family. Its name means "first horned face." Protoceratops had a large face and a small neck **frill**. This dinosaur was about the size of a pig, although it weighed two tons.

Its head was so heavy that it had to walk on all four feet most of the time. Baby Protoceratops had small neck frills. The frills grew quickly as Baby chewed tough plants and exercised its muscles. Baby Protoceratops was cared for by its parents in a nest, just like birds are, until it grew big enough to follow the herd.

Protoceratops had a parrot-like beak, several hundred teeth, and strong face muscles. It could eat almost anything that grew, even wood.

Protoceratops eggs were the first dinosaur eggs ever discovered. It was then, in 1922, that scientists first learned that dinosaurs laid eggs.

16

DIMORPHODON
(dye-MORF-uh-don)

Dimorphodon means "two-formed tooth." This **carnivore** had large, leathery wings and a tremendous head. Dimorphodon was one of the earliest members of the **Pterosaur** family of flying reptiles. It had sharp teeth and a long, bony tail.

Dimorphodon was only three feet long, but its wingspan was almost six feet. It flew through the air by catching updrafts of gentle winds with its wings. Stronger winds could send it blowing off course.

Dimorphodon ate small mammals, which it caught by diving out of the sky and grabbing with its short, sharp claws. Even though it was a meat-eater itself, Dimorphodon often fell victim to larger carnivores.

Dimorphodon slept hanging upside-down from a tree, just like a bat.

18

TRICERATOPS
(try-SAIR-uh-tops)

Triceratops means "three-horned face." It had two horns that stuck out from above its eyes. These could be as long as three feet. Its third horn grew out of its nose, and was about one foot in length. These famous horns were not used for attack. They were only used for defense.

Triceratops was part of the Ceratopsian group of dinosaurs. It had a bony frill on its head that looked like an upside-down saddle. This plant-eater had a head that seemed too big for its body. Extra neck muscles helped support the tremendous weight of its head.

This dinosaur was well protected from attacks. Its frill and its thick, leathery skin acted as armor against enemies.

Triceratops was one of the last of the dinosaurs to ever roam the earth.

TYRANNOSAURUS REX
(tye-RAN-uh-sawr-us rex)

Its name means "king of the tyrant lizards." This giant carnivore was feared by all dinosaurs. It was the largest of the meat-eaters. It could grow to be 40 feet long and 18 feet tall. Tyrannosaurus Rex had a big tail that it used for balance as it lunged for its prey. It had very short arms.

Tyrannosaurus Rex had huge teeth that measured up to six inches in length. The teeth were flat and had a jagged edge, like a steak knife.

Tyrannosaurus Rex had a very large skull which enabled it to open its enormous jaws very wide. This allowed it to take extra big bites out of its **quarry**.

The jaws of Tyrannosaurus Rex were three feet long and held 60 teeth.

22

GLOSSARY

Alamosaurus—A 30-ton Sauropod first discovered in Texas.

Algoasaurus—A small Sauropod from South Africa whose thigh bone was only 19½ inches long. This was much smaller than most other Sauropods.

Ankylosaur—A family of heavily-armored, plant-eating dinosaurs.

Ankylosaurus—A heavily-armored, tank-like plant-eater.

Apatosaurus—Also called Brontosaurus, this was one of the largest Sauropods.

Carnivore—A meat-eating animal.

Ceratopsian—A group of plant-eating dinosaurs that had horns or frills on their heads.

Diplodocus—This Sauropod was the largest of all dinosaurs.

Fossils—Impressions left in the earth by animals or plants from another time.

Frill—A large bony plate that rested on the heads of Ceratopsian dinosaurs. It acted as protective armor.

Herbivore—A plant-eating animal.

Paleontologists—Scientists who study dinosaurs.

Pterosaur—Flying lizard.

Quarry—The victim of a hunter.

Sauropod—Four-legged, plant-eating dinosaurs. These gentle giants were the biggest of all the dinosaurs.

Spinosaurid—A large meat-eating dinosaur with long bones that jutted up from the spine.

Stegosaurus—A plate-backed herbivore that had bony spikes on its tail.

Titanosaurs—A type of Sauropod that had narrow skulls and high nostrils.

Triassic—The dinosaur age beginning 225 million years ago and ending 190 million years ago.

Vertebrae—Neck and spine bones.